# THIRD & HEAVEN